UKULELE JAMBOREE!

25 Sing-Along Songs to Cheer You Up!

MB22138

BY IAN WHITCOMB

MUSIC TYPESETTING: TIM EMMONS

FREE AUDIO AVAILABLE ONLINE!
VISIT: WWW.MELBAY.COM/22138

Visit us on the Web at www.melbay.com or www.billsmusicshelf.com

Contents and Audio Tracks

Vocals on tracks 1 & 14 by The Chorines (Amy Greenberg, Diane Kelber, Brett Stone, Theresa Gorton); track 7 by Ian & The Chorines; tracks 3 & 5 by Janet Klein and Ian; track 6 by Irving Kaufman; track 12 by Aileen Stanley; tracks 22 & 25 by Ian & Regina Whitcomb; track 24 by Charles W. Hamp.

A Welcome From The Author

This little songbook is a celebration of the spirit for use by ukulele entertainers and everybody else who wants to feel better in these often sad times of ours. There are no hymns or songs of praise as in a church, but the function is pretty much the same: the use of song to raise you out of yourself and onto another plateau where all is merry and bright. An alternative medicine to pills and the like.

I want you to use these songs like friendly weapons. Wield them gaily at gatherings—parties, concerts, restaurants, business meetings, railway stations, airports, political demonstrations. You'll spread happiness, contentment and peace wherever you sing them. If we only had an army of ukesters singing these numbers we could march into any troubles part of the globe and within moments every belligerent would lay down their arms and surrender. Soon all would be joining in the fun.

Now I'll admit that some of these songs may seem a little saucy and others may provoke a tear or two. But it'll be good healthy sauce and the tears will be a relief. We need the twin feelings of sunshine and shadow. Together they make us whole. A good decent well-built song, like refreshing food and drink, is one of the crucial ingredients in the stuff of life. It can see you through a crisis, it can lift you out of the grim or quotidian reality of this particular world.

A good song, taken like a train or plane, will convey us into the dreams we are made out of. On no account must we sit on our bottoms as if in a drear and dreadful concert hall, hushed and awe-struck as one of our musical betters batters at the pianoforte and all we are allowed to do is to applaud at the finish. And will it ever finish? And when it does finish we're not permitted to boo. This is passive art and I have no time for it!

Good and famous authors knew the power of song. The instant evocation conjured by a snatch of lyric—and we are back in a period, a feeling, a situation. Scott Fitzgerald, Frank O'Hara, T.S Eliot, and old James Joyce all quoted freely and easily when in need of a quick fix.

In this book are songs of the open road, of the camaraderie of the cocktail, of magic lands in Dixie where the Earth Mother waits with pecan pie and more, of the elixir of the common cough, of the pleasures of the party when fruity Teddy is hosting, of invigorating jazz dances such as the Sheep Dip, of little cowboys in need of sleep, of common-or-garden yellow birds that can magically bring back your dead father, of dancing at twilight with the mysterious love of your life. Nothing mundane here.

We end with "Till We Meet Again", a lulling and comforting old-time waltz, one of a clutch of songs in this book that your author hasn't written.

Pull out your ukuleles and follow the dancing print. If you want to hear my version on record then download and play along. I'm joined in "Ambling Along" and "Have A Martini" by the songbird Janet Klein & Her Parlour Boys. "That's How I Need You" is sung by Irving Kaufman, "Apple Blossom Time" by Aileen Stanley, and "Rose Of The Rio Grande" by Charles Hamp. These are vintage recordings from old radio show transcriptions.

Arm yourself with a tuneful uke. I play a soprano Martin that I bought new in 1968. I recommend Flukes for those who haven't deep pockets. Be careful of any uke offered in the $25 range. They give ukes a bad name.

Remember that the uke was devised by the nautical Portuguese as an accompaniment for singing. It is not a high-lass concert instrument. Playing Wagner, Bach or 100mph flights of bumblebees is for wowing certain masses. It seems expensive stuff but in fact it's cheap---it's a merely a common road race. Uke music is song and perhaps a little dance. A Caper.

And Uke Can Do It!

Ian Whitcomb

Laugh!

A Bucolic Romp

Ha! Ha! Ha!

Words & Music by Ian Whitcomb

I Love You

Waltz

Words & Music by Ian Whitcomb

Ambling Along

Bracing Outdoor Stroll

Words & Music by Ian Whitcomb

F 7
D 7
G 7
Smil - ing 'cos we got no stocks or shares
Cmi
E♭mi6
F 7
A   B♭ Dmi
C 7
We've no need for te - le - phones   All we hear are bird - ie bell tones
C 9
C 7
Cmi
F 7
B♭ E♭mi B♭
stamp foot
Twee-ty tweet tweet-y tweet   twee - ty tweet tweet   Got no mo-ney   Got no cares!

The All-American Hand Dance

A Hand Routine (Includes the Wave)

Words & Music by Ian Whitcomb

F7
A7
B♭
That's   the   All - Am - er - i - can   Hand   Dance
B♭9
E♭
Ges - tures   can   cool 'em   The   world   we   can   save   And
C9
F7
if   that   don't   fool   'em   We've   al - ways   got   the   wave
DO A SYNCHRONIZED WAVE
A°7
B♭
But   if   your   en - em -
B♭
G7
ies   still   lin - ger   Then   you've   al - ways   got   the   fin - ger
C7
F7
B♭
That's   the   Un - i - ver - sal   Hand   Dance!

Have A Martini!

A Tipsy Waltz

Words & Music by Ian Whitcomb

49
FINE
Bb G7 C7 F7 Bb Eb Bb
ti - ni   And let life be - gin

57
G7 C7
I can eas-ily prove that   I can hold my liq-uor   No quo-ta-tion ev-er   proves to be a stick-er

61
F7 Bb A7 Ab7
"Pe - ter Pi - per picked a   pick - led pep - per - corn" How's   that?

65
G7 C7
"Sis-ter Sus-ie's sew-ing   shirts for sol-diers" and then   "Ma-ry had a lit-tle   lamb" You see, I told ya,

69
F7 Bb
I can shay mosht al - most   an - y-think,   Oh   drat!   There's

73
Gb7 Bb C7 F7 D.S. al Fine
on - ly one pro - per way out   So fill up your glas-ses and   shout:

That's How I Need You

Words by Joe McCarthy/Music byAl Piantadosi

C   C°7   C
ros - es   need   their   fra - grance_______   Like a
Cadd9   E7   F
sweet - heart   needs   a   kiss_______   Like the
Dmi   G7   Dmi7   G7
sum - mer   needs   the   sun - shine_______   Like a
Dmi7   G7   C
lad - die   needs   a   miss_______   Like a
Cadd9   C°7   C
bro - ken   heart   needs   glad - ness_______   Like the
Cadd9   C7   F
flow - ers   need   the   dew_______   Like a
A+   A7   D7
ba - by   needs   its   mo - - ther -
G6   G7   C
That's   How   I   Need   You!_______

Cottage By The Sea

Moderate Foxtrot

Words & Music by Ian Whitcomb

Sea built for you and me we'll be fan-cy free __________ Ro-ses 'round the
door, love on ev-ery floor who could ask for more __________ Scent-ed breez-es
blow, tink-ling wa-ters flow Bird-ies hop up on my win-dow sill __________
trill-ing such thrill-ing mel-o-dies __________ (They tell of love sent from a-bove) When the whippor-
wills from the gol-den hills ban-ish all our ills __________ E-ven-tide I
come, when my work is done. when the west-ern sun is set-ting.
She's get-ting din-ner read - y: I'm get-ting feath-er bed-dy

Love Never Makes A Mistake

Waltz

Words & Music by Ian Whitcomb

G9
G7
Love ne - ver gets it all wrong
C7
C°7
C7
C°7
C7
You said the mo - ment you met me
F
Ab°7
Gmi
C7
Life was as sweet as a song
F
F°7
F
D7
Ev - en tho' friends had their doubts and
Gmi
D7
Gmi
Said you'd be tro - uble and strife
G9
F
D7
Love nev - er makes a mistake, so We'll
Gmi
C7
F
be to - geth - er for life

In Tennessee

Foxtrot

Words & Music by Ian Whitcomb

F
G 7
C 7
A 7
D 7
G 7
A♭°7
F
D 7
G 7
C 7
F
stroll a - gain In a leaf - y lane Down Nash-ville___ way and to
be once more in the gen - eral store Where I will___ say:
"Come on Ba - by let me hear you sing, ___ 'Cuz I'm gonna buy you ___ a wedding ___ ring!" and we'll
set - tle down in a one horse town in Ten-nes - see!

I'm Gonna Live While I'm Living
('Cause I'm Gonna Be A Long Time Dead)

One-step ragtime feel

Words & Music by Ian Whitcomb

G7
29
I'm gon - na drink the town dry
C7
33
Ami
C7
I'm gon - na take down my trou - sers and
F
37
E7
Ami
C7
make all the wo - men say "My!"
F7
41
B♭
And while you bor - ing folks are tucked up in your bunk
G7
45
C7
I'll honk my horn and shout out "Look Ma, I'm drunk"! 'Cause
F
49
D7
I'm Gon - na Live While I'm liv - ing 'Cause I'm
G7
53
Ami
C7
F
gon - na be a long time dead

Let's Have A Jolly Good Cough

A Seasonal Waltz

Words & Music by Ian Whitcomb

Second Chorus:
Now you're happy and free from phlegm, you've had a jolly good cough
Tell the people! Encourage them to carry our message aloft
Tell the world it can celebrate if we all just expectorate
With the stuff from our throat we can go float a boat
Let's Have A Jolly Good Cough!

Apple Blossom Time

Chorus

I'll be with you in Ap - ple Blos - som Time
I'll be with you to change your name to mine
One day in May I'll come and say
"Hap - py the bride the sun shines on to - day"
What a won - der - ful wed - ding there will be
What a won - der - ful day for you and me
Church bells will chime You will be mine in
Ap - ple Blos - som Time

The Clap-Clap Crew

Medium tempo foxtrot

26

G7
G+ C C#°7 G7
27 We see some-bo-dy you don't know Off we go with a Clap! Clap! Clap!
C
C7
F
31 Why don't you join us in our Clap! Clap! Clap! Why won't you join us tell us please?
D7
C A7
D7
G7
C
35 We can't hear you We won't hear you When we're go - ing Clap! Clap! Clap!

Do The Sheep Dip

This page has been left blank
to avoid awkward page turns.

Dancing In The Twilight

Tango

Words & Music by Ian Whitcomb

G6 G Emi7 Bb°7 D7
Twi - light Once more I feel O. K. When you spread your
D7 B7
love - light I'm just a slave in your sway
E7 A9 A7 Bb°7
Let me stay won't you let me sway 'til the morn - ing But here's that
Ami7 D7 G
warn - ing sign And once more down the hole we go!

Shiny Shoes

Words and Music by Ian Whitcomb

Two-beat feel
Verse
Cmi   G 7   Cmi   G 7   Cmi
Oi Vay Vat a fuss! Since she got off the bus Our
Fmi   C 7   Fmi   C 7   Fmi
sheet is in a stir And all be - cause of her
G 7   Cmi
Once we were ko - sher and ob - ser - vant
A mi7b5   D 7   Gmi   Bb7
Now we're her ser - vant and we cry:
Eb
Shi - ny Shoes! How she loves to wear her
F 7
Shi - ny Shoes 'Cos they make her lose those
Bb7   Eb   C 7
pes - ky blues Her Shi - ny Shoes
F 7   Bb7   Bb+
Watch what hap - pens to her When I strap 'em to her

Verse 2: I vos so upset
But then I made a bet
That this girl I could get
To do the right thing yet
I married Ruby and I tamed her
When babies came they look the same as her
They all had...

Chorus 2: Shiny Shoes!
How they love to wear their Shiny Shoes
'Cos they make them lose those pesky blues
Those Shiny Shoes
Watch what happens to them
When they strap 'em to 'em
See them dance!
They'll hoochie coochie 'til the dawn comes thund-'ring through
And if you play it right
They just might
Trip the light fantastic with you

You Cannot Go Away

Inspirational Waltz

Words & Music by Ian Whitcomb

29
Fmi B♭7 B♭mi6 E♭7
Give me the or - der to land________ I
33
A♭ D♭
know you would have liked her I wish you two had met Please
37
A♭ Fmi B♭7 E♭ E♭+
grant me just one mo - ment To stay with you yet But
41
C7 Fmi F7 B♭7 E♭7
time claims ev' - ry bo - dy There's no - thing but de - cay You
45
A♭ Cmi A♭7 F7 B♭7 E♭7 A♭
both must stay with - in me You Can - not Go A - way!

Sophie

Words & Music by Abner Silver

Fast and Saucy Strut

Chorus 2: I go so far with Sophie on Sophie's sofa and Sophie goes so far with me
Ev-'ry time I look in- to her eyes I'm done
She's got those kind of eyes- Oh Mother save your son!
Oh I know that she trusts me just like a brother she likes my company
Oh Mother! Mother! Mother! Your son's a mixer
Take down the mazuzeh I'm bringing home a shiksa
I go so far with Sophie on Sophie's sofa and Sophie goes so far with me

The Yellow Bird

Yel-low Bird looked sad and droo - py In fact I thought I saw a tear____ So I
clam-bered up the tree quite quick - ly And had a whis-per in his ear____
asked if I could see my fa - ther who died in Nine-teen Six-ty Two____ The
bir-die flapped his wings so brisk - ly And said he'd see what he could do____
Then that night my fath-er came____ and we chat-ted like we'd nev-er done be - fore
I ex-plained I think he un-der-stood____And in the morn-ing he was there no more____ Well I
searched a-round my L. A. gar - den And hid-den in the old oak____ tree I
found a scrib-bled note from that bir - die He said "I'm glad that you be-lieve in me"____

I Love You 'Cause You're Fun To Be With

40

Ami   F7
Oth - er lov - ers smooch in the gloom____ but you
A7   D7   G7
light up a room____ with your sweet sun - ny smile____
C7   F
You trip the light fan - tas - tic o - ver the floor____
D7   G7
You send the dan - cers cra - zy yell - ing for more____ But
C   Dmi   C°7   C   Dmi   E7   Ami   Fmi   C
on - ly I know what lies in store____ we'll have
D7   D7b5   G7   C
fun with - out laugh - ing to - night!____

Go To Sleep Little Cowboy

Western Jog Trot

Words & Music: Unknown. Arranged by Ian Whitcomb

43

This page has been left blank
to avoid awkward page turns.

Teddy's At It Again!
A Jollity March

Words & Music by Ian Whitcomb

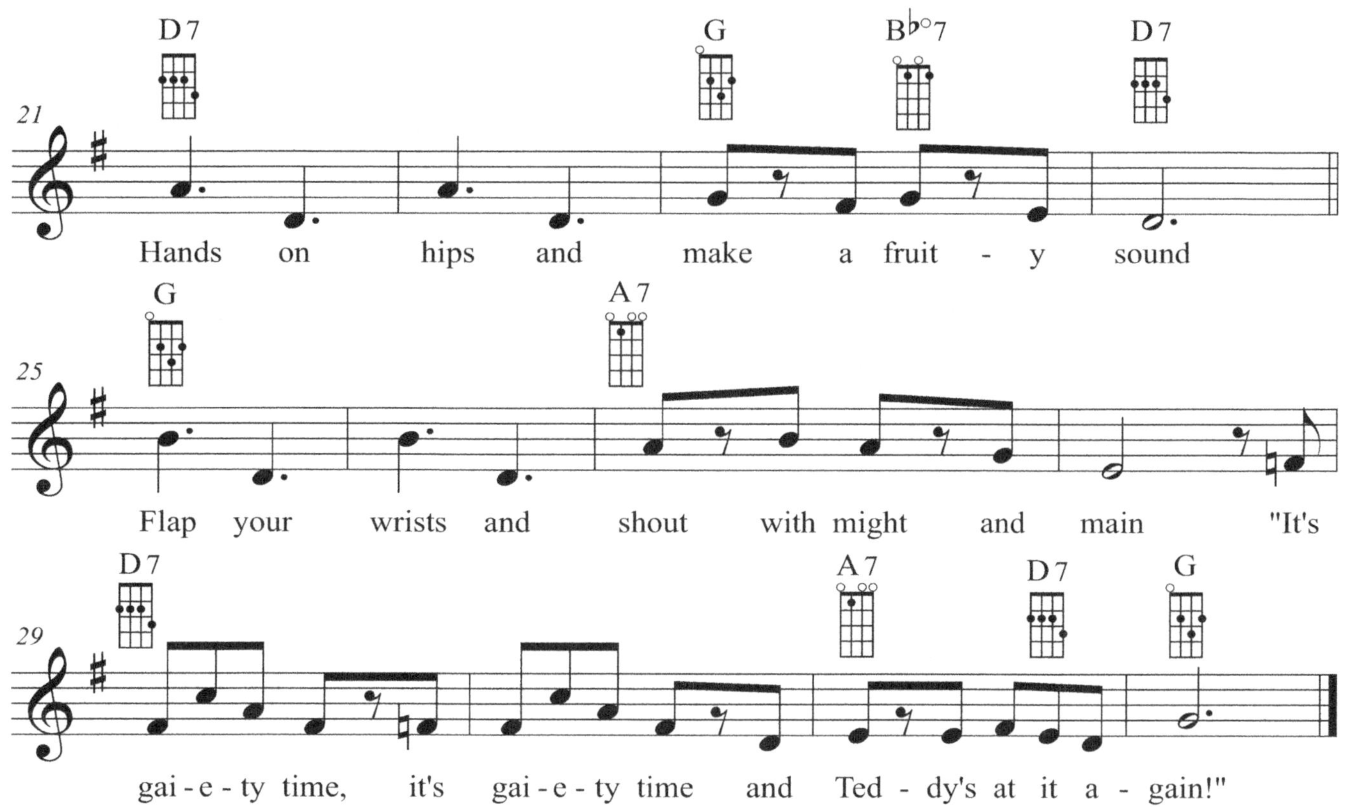

Verse #2: Teddy got arrested and they threw him in the clink
But you can be certain that his spirits didn't sink
Soon he ran the entertainment and at Christmas time
The good and the bad- every lad-
Sang out this seasonal rhyme:

Chorus: Bend down! Hands up!
Waggle it around!
Hands on hips and make a fruity sound
Flap your wrists and shout with might and main
"It's gaiety time, it's gaiety time and Teddy's at it again!"

Verse #3: When Ted got out he took a trip out to the Middle East
He filled his trunks with juicy hunks- a real right royal feast!
When he landed on the rocks in wild Afghanistan
He shouted out loud to the crowd and all the Taliban:

Chorus: Bend down! Hands up!
Waggle it around!
Hands on hips and make a fruity sound
Flap your wrists and shout with might and main
"It's gaiety time, it's gaiety time and Teddy's at it again!"

It's Gotta Be You

Langorous Swing

Words & Music by Ian Whitcomb

D 7   D+   G   Emi
21
is - n't all the glitz____ Like din - ing at the Ritz____ That
A 7   D 7
25
fills me with a glow which nev - er quits____________ It is-sn't the
G 6   D+   Gma7   D+   G   B♭°7
29
dia-monds it is-n't the lob-sters it is-n't the chance____ to meet rock stars and
G   G 7   C   E 7   A mi
32
mob-sters____ that makes me want to cud-dle you and coo____________ It is - n't ma-
A 7   G   E 7
37
ter - i - al____ that makes me e - ther - e - al____ You hav-en't a
A   D 7   G
39
bean I'd bet - ter come clean It's Got - ta be You!

Rose Of The Rio Grande

Chorus
A7
Rose Of The Ri - o Grande
D7
Rose of the bor - der land
G7
One word then hand in hand We'll
C Ami6 E A E B7 E7
leave the prea - cher's side room Hap - py lit - tle bride and bride - groom
A7
O - ver those hills of sand
D7
I've got our love nest planned
G7 C9 A7
You claim it I'll name it
D7 G7 C Fmi C
Rose of Ri - o - Grande

Till We Meet Again
Eternal Waltz

Lyric by Raymond B. Egan   **Music by Richard Whiting**

A 7   D 7   A#°
Down in lov - ers lane my dear - ie
G   D 7
Wed - ding bells will ring so mer - ri - ly
D 7   G   G 7
Ev - 'ry tear will be a mem - o - ry So
C   G   G 7   E 7
wait and pray each night for me
A 7   D 7   G   C   G
Till we meet a - gain

IAN WHITCOMB

Ian, a British Invader of the 1960s, is a respected historian of popular music. He helped revive interest in the ukulele via his early recordings dating from 1965. He and Ukie have been seen on Johnny Carson's "Tonight Show", "Today", "Merv Griffin", "American Bandstand", "Where The Action Is". Watch him in these shows on You Tube. Find out more than enough about him at his website --*ianwhitcomb.com*—and at wikipedia.

This book is the 4th in a series of uke- friendly songbooks that Ian has had published by Mel Bay Publications. The others are: *"Ukulele Heaven"* , *"Uke Ballads"*," *The Cat's Meow"* and *"The Ian Whitcomb Songbook"* .

Made in the USA
Monee, IL
07 July 2026